Sociology in Pictures: Theories an

Self-Study and Teacher's C....

Michael Haralambos
with Wendy Hope

Contents

Published by Collins Educational
An imprint of HarperCollins Publishers, 77-85 Fulham Palace Road, Hammersmith, London W6 8JB

© Michael Haralambos, 2013
10 9 8 7 6 5 4 3 2 1
ISBN 978-0-00-754267-3

British Library Cataloguing in Publication Data.
A catalogue record for this publication is available from the British Library.

Typography and design by John A Collins and Matthew Waring-Collins

Printed and bound in the UK by www.waringcollins.com

QUESTIONS AND ANSWERS

Q1 *How does the idea of culture help to explain the behaviour in the top two pictures?*

A1 Culture is the learned, shared behaviour of members of society. People see the world in terms of their culture and act in accordance with the norms which form a part of that culture. In the first picture, the North American feels uncomfortable and retreats because the appropriate conversational space defined by his culture has been invaded. And the South American advances because he feels too far away in terms of the conversational distance defined by his culture.

In the second picture, the missionary feels embarrassed because the norms of his culture define bare female breasts in public as unacceptable. He takes what he sees as appropriate action and imports bras. However, from their point of view, the women have no such qualms about bare breasts. They define the bras as suitable headgear and take appropriate action.

Q2 *How does counting coup reflect the high value placed on bravery by Plains tribes?*

A2 It places the person counting coup in a dangerous situation because he is striking an armed enemy with a wooden stick. Risking life in this way is seen as a brave act. As such, it brings honour and prestige to the person counting coup.

Q3 *Norms are sometimes backed by laws. How is this shown by polygyny in Western society?*

A3 Polygyny is considered to be wrong by most people in Western society. This view is supported by the law which refers to it as bigamy and defines it as illegal. The norm is monogamy – marriage between two people – and it is backed by the law.

EVALUATION

Culture is a useful concept. It helps make sense of the vast range of human behaviour. It shows that what appears nonsense to people in one society makes perfect sense to people in another. It shows that our actions are, to a large extent, based on what we learn and what we share with members of our society.

The idea of culture was developed by American anthropologists studying the norms and values of Native American peoples. It is particularly applicable to small-scale societies where everybody shares the same culture. Many of today's large-scale societies are described as multicultural. For example, the UK and the USA have ethnic populations which, to some extent, have their own cultures. The term *subculture* is sometimes used to describe such cultures. People with their own subculture share many aspects of the mainstream culture but have some distinctive norms and values.

SOCIAL CONTROL

QUESTIONS AND ANSWERS

Q1 Here are two views of the role of the police in society

    a) **They benefit society as a whole.**

    b) **They serve the rich and powerful.**

    Give a brief argument to support each view.

A1 a) The police enforce the law and maintain order. This benefits all members of society.

    b) The police keep the working class in their place. They also prevent demonstrations and protests from threatening the power and privileges of those at the top.

Q2 **Suggest why informal methods of social control are important.**

A2 They act as a deterrent to prevent deviance from norms and rules occurring in the first place. For example, informal methods such as public surveillance can deter crime.

Q3 **How can religion be seen as a mechanism of social control?**

A3 Religion can support institutions in society and, by doing so, reinforce their control over behaviour. The picture shows archbishops giving their blessing to the coronation of a monarch. During the Middle Ages, European monarchs ruled by 'divine right'. This stated that their right to rule came directly from God. As a result, those who disobeyed royal commands were going against the will of God. This strengthened the ruler's control over their subjects.

The norms and values of society are reinforced if they are supported by religious commandments. Deviating from them becomes a sin. In this respect, religion can be seen as a mechanism of social control.

Q4 **In which ways can the family be seen as a mechanism of social control?**

A4 Social control is largely based on learning society's norms and values. The family plays an important part in this process. In most societies it has the main responsibility for teaching young children what is acceptable. And it does this when children are at their most impressionable.

The family has a range of sanctions to reward conformity to norms and values and to punish deviance. It can reward with praise, privileges and approval and punish with displeasure, withdrawing privileges and with disapproval. In teaching and enforcing norms and values, the family can be seen as a powerful mechanism of social control.

EVALUATION

Social control is an important concept. It is used by a variety of sociologists working from a number of different perspectives. Some see it as the basis for social order, as essential for the survival of the social system and generally beneficial for society as a whole. Others see it as an oppressive and coercive mechanism used by a wealthy and powerful minority to keep the majority in their place. It is sometimes seen as a means of disguising oppression and justifying the position of those at the top.

QUESTIONS AND ANSWERS

Q1 *Why did Marx believe that feudalism and capitalism are based on exploitation?*

A1 Exploitation means using others for your own gain at their expense. According to Marx, under feudalism the land is the main force of production. It is owned by lords and farmed by serfs – the landless peasants. The serfs produce the wealth but much of it is taken from them by the lords in the form of taxes and the produce of the land.

In capitalist industrial society, the forces of production – the factories and raw materials – are owned by the capitalists. The workers produce the wealth but much of it is taken away from them in the form of profits by capitalists.

Marx argued that in both feudal and capitalist society the subject class produced the wealth but most of it was taken from them by the ruling class. As a result, Marx saw the ruling class exploiting the subject class.

Q2 *How might the ruling class ideology reinforce and justify ruling class power?*

A2 According to Marx, ruling class ideology is a set of beliefs which present a false and distorted picture of society. In doing so, it disguises the true nature of class society and conceals the exploitation on which it is based. It goes further by presenting a positive and, at times, a rosy view of society. For example, it pictures capitalism as a fair and reasonable system and promotes the view that we live in a free and democratic society. As a result, ruling class ideology reinforces and justifies ruling class power.

Q3 *How can the state be seen as an instrument of the ruling class?*

A3 In terms of what it does and what it does not do, Marx argued that the state supports the ruling class. First, what it does. The state passes laws which make legal the private ownership of industry and the right of owners to any profits which might be made. Governments support private industry, arguing that it produces wealth, creates jobs and provides exports, all of which are good for the nation as a whole. Second, what the state does not do. It does not seriously question the morality of capitalism, it does not seriously consider alternatives to the capitalistic economic system. In terms of what it does and does not do, the state can be seen as an instrument of the ruling class.

Q4 *How did Marx see religion?*

A4 Marx took a very dim view of religion. He saw it as fantasy, illusion, false consciousness. He compared its effect to that of opium – an hallucinatory drug which he saw as producing misapprehension, mistaken perception, figments of the imagination. And, like opium, he saw religion as producing false happiness, delusions of pleasure. In doing so, it eased the pain of exploitation and oppression. This dulled and depressed the motivation to rebel against the system. To Marx, religion was a harmful concoction which blinded humankind to truth and reality.

Q5   *Why did Marx believe that communism would produce an equal society?*

A5   Marx believed that inequality in class society occurred when a minority own the forces of production. In a communist society, the forces of production are owned by all the people – they are communally owned. Marx believed that this would result in an equal society. There would be no ruling class and subject class. The state would 'wither away' as it represents a minority ruling over a majority. The people would govern themselves.

EVALUATION

For many, Marx's vision of a future society has been inspirational. For others, it is a dangerous fantasy. Here are some of the criticisms of Marx's views and the responses of his supporters.

- The class system is more complex than Marx's description. A growing middle class has emerged between capitalists and workers. Marx recognised the existence of other classes, for example small business owners, but saw them as relatively unimportant compared to the two main classes.

- Marx's predictions have not materialised. The ruling class has not been overthrown. A classless society has not arisen from the collapse of Western capitalism. The revolutions which led to communism have occurred in non-capitalist societies.

- The communist societies of Eastern Europe and the Soviet Union did not produce the equality and freedom of Marx's vision. They were governed by powerful ruling elites and there were few, if any, signs of movement towards equality. Communism collapsed in the late 1980s and early 1990s to be replaced by capitalism and a move towards democracy.

- Marx has been accused of economic determinism – of seeing human behaviour as shaped by economic forces. Marx did see economic factors as primary but not the only factors shaping behaviour. In his words, 'Men make history but not under circumstances of their own choosing'.

- Marx has been seen as a preoccupied with class inequality, and ignoring other forms of inequality such as those based on gender and ethnicity.

- Despite the many criticisms of Marx, his ideas remain important and influential. They have produced new and distinctive analyses in every area of sociology, from religion and education to gender and crime.

- Marx's views of ideology and false consciousness have provided valuable insights. And his critical views have helped to open our eyes to the inequalities and delusions which exist in today's society.

BIOGRAPHY

Karl Marx (1818-1883) was born into a wealthy middle-class family in Prussia, then part of the German Confederation. He studied philosophy, law, history and languages at the Universities of Bonn and Berlin. He wrote for various radical, left-wing newspapers in Cologne and Paris. He moved to Paris in 1843 where he met his lifetime friend and collaborator, Frederick Engels. He was exiled from both Germany and France for his revolutionary views and moved to London in 1849 where he spent the rest of his life. Marx wrote an enormous amount of material. Probably his most accessible publication is *The Communist Manifesto* (1848), written with Engels when both were fairly young, enthusiastic and bursting with ideas.

ALIENATION

QUESTIONS AND ANSWERS

Q1 *What does Marx mean when he describes workers in capitalist society as dehumanised?*

A1 Marx argued that workers in capitalist society are alienated from their work. He believed that work is the way for people to express their true humanity. If they are alienated from work they are dehumanised – they are unable to express their humanity, they cannot express their human essence. As a result, in Marx's words, 'the worker does not fulfil himself, has a feeling of misery, is mentally debased'.

Q2 *Why does Marx refer to work in capitalist society as 'forced labour'?*

A2 Marx argued that workers are forced to work for capitalists in order to earn money to survive. They are not free to work for themselves and everybody else. They are employed as individuals, they have little or no say in the matter, they are wage slaves working under the yoke, servitude and domination of their capitalist masters.

Q3 *According to Marx, why are workers alienated from each other?*

A3 Marx believed that in an ideal communist society people would work both for themselves and everybody else – for the common good. However, under capitalism this was not possible. People worked as individual employees. They competed for jobs in the labour market. They worked to earn money only for themselves and their families. As a result, they were alienated from their fellow workers.

EVALUATION

Marx presented a very positive vision of work in communist society. His critics, however, have tended to see it as wishful thinking. They point to the former communist countries of Eastern Europe where there was little indication of fulfilled workforces producing goods and services for themselves and the community as a whole.

Instead, it appeared that a self-interested governing elite controlled the workforce and received a disproportionate share of the goods produced. However, in Marx's defence, these countries were a long way from the communist societies he looked forward to.

More recently, Marxists have developed Marx's ideas of alienation. For example, in *One Dimensional Man* Herbert Marcuse (1972) argued that work under capitalism remains 'exhausting, stupefying, inhuman slavery'. And leisure involves 'modes of relaxation which soothe and prolong this stupefaction' resulting in 'euphoria in unhappiness'. Exploitation and alienation become more bearable as living standards improve and people satisfy 'false needs' by consuming material goods.

EMILE DURKHEIM

QUESTIONS AND ANSWERS

Q1 *Suggest some of the 'essential similarities which social life demands'. Show how they might provide a basis for cooperation and social unity.*

A1 Effective communication can be seen as a basis for cooperation and social unity. A shared language can be seen as necessary for this. In addition, shared norms, beliefs and values can be seen as 'essential similarities'. If norms, beliefs and values differ, this may produce conflict and division. People are more likely to feel a part of society and more likely to cooperate if they feel that they are living with people like themselves.

Q2 *Suggest how families, schools and religions might work together for the benefit of society as a whole.*

A2 If families, schools and religions transmit the same norms, values and beliefs, then the 'essential similarities which social life demands' are more likely to be produced. In the first instance, if families socialise their children in terms of the same basic norms, values and beliefs, and these are later reinforced by the teachings of schools and religions, then this will contribute to cooperation, social order, a collective conscience and social solidarity. The various parts of society will then be in harmony, reinforcing each other and benefiting the social system as a whole.

EVALUATION

Durkheim is sometimes regarded as the first *real* sociologist who provided the framework for the modern discipline. He is sometimes seen as the first *functionalist*, so-called because one of his main concerns was the analysis of the *functions* of the various parts of society – that is, the contributions the various parts make to society as a whole. In this respect, Durkheim used an *organic analogy*, comparing society with an organism. In each case, an understanding of their functioning can be provided by examining how their parts contribute to the well-being of the whole.

Durkheim argued that society has certain basic needs – such as social solidarity and a collective conscience. If these needs are not met, then self-interest will be 'the only ruling force' and each individual will find themselves 'in a state of war with every other'. To prevent this, Durkheim argues, 'society has to be present in the individual'.

A major part of Durkheim's sociology is to look at how people's behaviour is shaped by the requirements, by the basic needs, of the social system. Critics argue that this view of society shaping behaviour largely ignores the degree to which people construct their own society and direct their own actions.

A second criticism states that Durkheim fails to give sufficient weight to the possibility that the norms and values of society may primarily benefit a ruling class or ruling elite rather than society as a whole.

BIOGRAPHY

Emile Durkheim (1858-1917) was born in Epinal in north-eastern France. He began his teaching career in the Department of Philosophy at the University of Bordeaux in 1887. His main responsibility was teaching courses on moral education. He also taught the first course in social science given by a French university. In 1902, he moved to the Sorbonne in Paris where he was appointed the first Professor of Education and Sociology in 1913. Durkheim was determined to establish sociology as a scientific discipline which he outlined in *The Rules of Sociological Method* (1895). His other major publications included *The Division of Labour in Society* (1893), *Suicide: A Study in Sociology* (1897) and *The Elementary Forms of Religious Life* (1912).

ANOMIE

QUESTIONS AND ANSWERS

Q1   *Use the idea of anomie to suggest reasons for the contentment and discontentment of the two couples in the first picture.*

A1   There is a ceiling on the desires and expectations of the first couple. They appear to have satisfied their desires and met their expectations in terms of the limits placed upon them. They are not experiencing anomie. As a result, they are contented.

There is a ceiling on the desires and expectations of the first couple. They appear to have satisfied their desires and met their expectations in terms of the limits placed upon them. They are not experiencing anomie. As a result, they are contented.

The second couple are experiencing anomie. There is no ceiling on their desires and expectations, no limits to their wants and hopes. In Durkheim's words, 'Reality seems valueless by comparison with the dreams of fevered imagination'. The second couple are discontented because they cannot satisfy their unlimited desires.

Q2   *Suggest why anomie might increase in times of boom and bust.*

A2   Periods of rapid economic change tend to disrupt society. Old norms break down and new ones have yet to replace them. In this situation, anomie or normlessness tends to develop.

In times of boom – rapidly increasing prosperity – people's lives can radically change. Their standard of living may greatly improve, they may move house, change jobs or give up work. They are no longer restrained by traditional norms, no longer embedded in their former lifestyle. As a result, they may be cast adrift and in limbo. The unlimited desires of anomie bring dissatisfaction, no matter how wealthy and successful they become.

In times of bust – economic recession – people's lives can also change rapidly. They may lose their house, job, security and sense of well-being. They too experience a situation of anomie – they are cast adrift and in limbo without traditional norms to govern their life.

In times of boom and bust, anomie is particularly acute. People tend to live in a moral vacuum, their lives unregulated. As a result, they are more prone to suicide.

EVALUATION

Despite being over 100 years old, Durkeim's concerns about modern society still seem fresh and relevant. Like many of today's sociologists, he saw a rise in individualism, an increase in the pace of social change, a lack of normative regulation and a decline in social integration. And many of the results of anomie – dissatisfaction, rootlessness and insecurity – are often identified as features of contemporary society by today's sociologists.

QUESTIONS AND ANSWERS

Q1 *Give two norms and two values that parents usually teach to their children. How do they teach these norms and values?*

A1 Norms include table manners, greetings and appropriate dress. Values include politeness, caring for others and respecting property. Children are taught by parents' example, by games they play and stories they are read, and by sanctions – rewards and punishments for 'good' and 'bad' behaviour.

Q2 *How does religion reinforce society's norms and values?*

A2 Religious beliefs are usually backed by an all-powerful, all-knowing, supernatural being. As a result, religion can exert a strong influence over its followers. It offers rewards for those who act in terms of its commandments – for example, eternal happiness in heaven – and punishments for those who do not – for example, eternal misery in hell. If religion reflects society's norms and values, then its teachings will reinforce them.

Q2 *How might examinations and assessments teach young people to achieve as individuals?*

A2 Young people are examined and assessed as individuals, not as a team. Their achievements as students are largely judged on the basis of their own performance. As a result, they learn to achieve as individuals.

Q2 *Explain the functionalist argument that unequal occupational rewards – in terms of income, power and status – benefit society as a whole.*

A2 Functionalists argue that some occupations are more important than others for the well-being of society. If this is the case, then a mechanism which ensures that these occupations are filled with the most talented and hardworking people will benefit society as a whole. This mechanism is unequal occupational rewards. Functionalists believe people will compete for the most highly rewarded jobs and that the most talented and hardworking will win through.

EVALUATION

Like Durkheim, functionalists assume that society has basic needs which must be met if it is to survive. These include social order and social integration. Shared norms and values are seen to meet these needs. And various parts of society are seen to transmit and reinforce these norms and values.

Functionalists often start with the question: What is the function of a particular part of society? In other words: What does it contribute to the well-being of society as a whole? Critics argue that this approach encourages researchers to look for positive contributions and to assume that various parts of society have beneficial functions. As a result, they tend to ignore possible negative effects or 'dysfunctions'. For example, social inequality can be seen as serving the interests of those at the top, as exploiting those at the bottom, and producing discord, division and conflict.

.

QUESTIONS AND ANSWERS

Q1 *According to Durkheim, social solidarity is one of the main requirements for an ordered society. How does he see religion functioning in Aboriginal society to promote social solidarity?*

A1 The totem is both a sacred symbol and the emblem of the clan. If the symbols representing supernatural power and the clan are the same, then this suggests that people are worshipping both. In doing so they are strengthening social solidarity. By coming together in the highly charged atmosphere of collective worship, they are reinforcing social unity.

Q2 *Apply Malinowski's ideas about the functions of religion to other situations – for example, warfare and illness.*

A2 Religion is often directed to situations which involve danger and where the outcome is in doubt. Such situations produce anxiety and insecurity. Religion can reduce these feelings by offering the support of supernatural powers. This can be seen when troops pray before a battle and by prayers said for recovery from a serious illness.

EVALUATION

Support for these functions of religion is provided by their application in a range of different societies and situations. For example, national flags and religion are often linked in ceremonies such as the inauguration of the US President. And religion is directed towards similar circumstances in a variety of societies, for example illness.

BIOGRAPHY

Born in Poland, Bronislaw Malinowski (1884-1942) became a British citizen. From 1915-1918, he studied the Trobriand Islanders who lived on small coral islands off the coast of New Guinea. He became Chairman of the Anthropology Department at the London School of Economics and in his last years was Professor of Anthropology at Yale University in the USA.

MAX WEBER

QUESTIONS AND ANSWERS

Q1   **Briefly outline the beliefs of 'ascetic Protestantism'.**

A1   Work is a religious calling. A godly person is hard-working and practices severe self-discipline. They reject pleasures and luxuries which they believe bring sorrow. Traditional fun and games such as the joys of Christmas are banned. Wasting time and money are frowned upon.

Q2   **Show how these beliefs may have led to Western industrial capitalism.**

A2   Weber argued that ascetic Protestantism produced the 'spirit of capitalism' which led to the development of industrial capitalism. Success in business showed that a person had not lost favour in the sight of God. And in John Wesley's words, 'Religion must necessarily produce hard work and discourage the wasting of money'. This is echoed by Benjamin Franklin who Weber saw as the embodiment of the spirit of capitalism. 'Remember that time is money. Always be employed in something useful.' With luxuries and frivolous entertainment banned, early capitalists had little else to do with their profits other than re-invest them in their businesses. All these factors focused the mind and activity on building a business, expanding that business, making profits and reinvesting those profits.

EVALUATION

From a Marxist viewpoint, religion, as a part of the superstructure, is shaped by the infrastructure – the economic base. Changes in the infrastructure will, therefore, lead to changes in religion. Weber accepts this can happen but argues that the reverse can also happen – that religion can lead to changes in the economy, as in the case of ascetic Protestantism. Thus, in Weber's view, social change can be led and directed by beliefs, ideas and world views.

Weber's study of the origins of capitalism has led to a large body of research. Some researchers have questioned his claim that ascetic Protestantism preceded capitalism. For example, Kautsky (1953) takes a Marxist position arguing that capitalism came first and ascetic Protestantism became the ideology of capitalists to legitimate their position and justify their wealth.

Weber's theory is know as social action theory. It is based on his view that human action is directed by meanings, in particular the way people see and understand the world, their 'world view'. To discover these meanings he used a method known as *verstehen* which is roughly translated as 'empathetic understanding'. Sociologists must attempt to see the world through the eyes of those they are studying. *The Protestant Ethic and the Spirit of Capitalism*, first published in 1904, is an example of the application of this approach.

BIOGRAPHY

Max Weber (1864-1920) was born into a wealthy, middle-class family in Erfurt, Germany. He had a difficult life with episodes of depression and conflict between his parents. His father was a successful bureaucrat and politician, his mother a devout Calvinist – an ascetic Protestant. The influence of both can be seen in his work.

Weber studied law, economics, history and philosophy at Heidelberg University and lectured at several top German universities. In 1910, he helped to found the German Sociological Society. His more important works include, *The Methodology of the Social Sciences* (1903), *The Protestant Ethic and the Spirit of Capitalism* (1904), *Economy and Society* (1910) and *The Sociology of Religion* (1916).

RATIONAL ACTION

QUESTIONS AND ANSWERS

Q1 *Compare the first two pairs of pictures. What aspects of instrumental rational action do they illustrate?*

A1 The first pair compares two views of the weather. The Hopi believe that the weather is controlled by supernatural powers. The modern weather forecaster sees the weather resulting from natural causes, in this case low pressure. From a rational viewpoint, there is no evidence to support the Hopi view. The weather forecaster bases her view on observations from the science of meteorology and on measurements and facts such as wind speed.

A similar comparison is provided by the pictures on medicine. The shaman believes that illness is caused by evil spirits and cured by removing those spirits. From a rational view, there is no evidence to support this belief. Modern medicine is based on measuring and assessing alternative ways of curing illness. In the words of the doctor, there is evidence to support the treatment she offers – the pills are 'tried, tested and proven to work'.

Q2 *How might the rational structure of bureaucracies help a business person to produce and make a profit from a new product? Refer to the picture in your answer.*

A2 Each of the departments shown in the picture might improve the product and increase the possibility of making a profit. Planning can develop the idea and assess the demand for the product. Design can create and evaluate alternative designs. Finance can cost the product and estimate its profitability. Marketing can produce advertising material and a marketing strategy. Legal can ensure that the product is not breaking laws such as health and safety legislation. Personnel can make sure that employees have the appropriate skills and experience. Each department has well-defined goals and clearly specified rules, and bases their assessments on precise calculations and relevant evidence.

Q3 *Outline Weber's worries about bureaucracy.*

A3 Weber refers to bureaucracy as an 'iron cage' which imprisons workers and restricts them in a variety of ways. Rules and regulations may prevent spontaneity, initiative and creativity. Workers may become 'specialists without spirit', without vitality and dynamism, trapped in their specialised routines, 'cogs in a bureaucratic machine'.

Q4 *What does Weber mean when he says that rational thinking has stripped the pursuit of wealth and material goods of its 'religious and ethical meaning'?*

A4 Weber believes that the pursuit of wealth and material goods has become an end in itself. Rational thinking leaves no room for religion and spirituality. It focuses on the most efficient means of reaching a goal. As the previous unit showed, ascetic Protestantism stated that wealth generated from business enterprise indicated that capitalists had not lost favour in the sight of God. These religious connotations have no place in instrumental rational action.

EVALUATION

Weber's views have been supported and developed by a number of sociologists. For example, in *Religion in a Secular Society* (1966), Bryan Wilson sees the rationalisation of Western society leading to a decline in religion. He argues that since religion is based on faith it is non-rational. As a result, its claim to truth cannot be tested by rational procedures.

In *The McDonaldisation of Society* (2007), George Ritzer argues that McDonald's 'fast-food model' has become the 'iron cage of rationality' in contemporary society. Like Weber's model of bureaucracy, it is efficient, predictable and governed by strict rules and regulations – even down to the weight of each burger. It crushes initiative and dehumanises workers. It is the latest example of Weber's instrumental rational action.

QUESTIONS AND ANSWERS

Q1   *Briefly compare Marx's (see Unit 3) and Weber's views of class.*

A1   Where Marx identified two main social classes, Weber identified four. Marx's classes were based on their relationship to the forces of production. The ruling class owned them, the subject class did not. Weber's classes were based on differences in market situation and the wealth and income they produced.

Q2   *Suggest how class differences produce differences in life chances – chances of obtaining things defined as desirable and avoiding things defined as undesirable.*

A2   People's chances of obtaining desirable things such as high living standards, quality housing and a long and healthy life are increased by the wealth and income that a high class position brings. Conversely, their chances of avoiding undesirable things, such as poverty, substandard housing and ill-health, are reduced the lower their position in the class system and the lower their wealth and income which results from this.

Q3   *Why do high class and high status often, but not always, go together?*

A3   Many people look up to the lifestyles and living standards that upper class wealth and income can provide. As a result, high class and high status often go together. However, the penniless aristocrat is often accorded high status because of their family background, taste and manners, despite their low class position. And the nouveau riche (newly rich) banker, despite their high class position, can lack the taste and manners that high status requires.

Q4   *What is the relationship between parties and class and status groups?*

A4   Parties sometimes represent class groups, as in the early years of the Labour Party when it was formed as a working-class party. Parties sometimes represent status groups, as in the case of women's and ethnic group associations. Parties often represent both class and status groups. For example, traditional trade unions had working-class memberships who shared a similar status. Parties sometimes represent neither class nor status groups as in the case of 'issue groups' such as Greenpeace and Friends of the Earth.

EVALUATION

Weber's views of the three dimensions of stratification – class, status and parties (power) – have informed all future classifications of social class. To some extent, sociologists have incorporated wealth and income, occupational status and power in their definitions of class systems.

Weber's views on life chances have had a similar influence. Weber stated, 'A class is a number of people having in common a specific causal component of life chances'. Since then, sociologists have conducted many studies on the relationship between class and life chances – for example, studies on the influence of class on educational opportunity and attainment.

THE CHICAGO SCHOOL

QUESTIONS AND ANSWERS

Q1 Robert Park saw the city rather than the library as the place for research. What evidence supports this statement?

A1 According to Park, 'real research' involves first-hand observation of real life. Park sent his students off the campus and on to the streets, into bars, into luxury hotels and cheap boarding houses.

Q2 Briefly describe the variations in zone rates of delinquency shown on the map.

A2 Zone 1 has the highest rate of delinquency. The rate then drops steadily to Zone 5, each zone having a lower rate than the previous one.

Q3 What may have caused social disorganisation in Zone 1?

A3 Zone 1 had a high population turnover. This resulted in an unsettled, unstable population and this contributed to social disorganisation. Zone 1 was an area of cultural heterogeneity – a variety of different cultures. This also contributed to social disorganisation. It tended to produce a number of separate communities rather than a single community with an overarching culture.

Q4 How might social disorganisation lead to high rates of crime?

A4 Informal mechanisms of social control are an important deterrent for crime (see Unit 2, Social Control). Examples include community disapproval and public surveillance. Social disorganisation results in weak informal mechanisms of social control. This can allow high rates of crime to develop.

Q5 The findings of Shaw and McKay's study are probably limited to a few American cities. Briefly discuss this view.

A5 A number of studies suggest that this might be the case. Morris's study indicates that high delinquency rates in Croydon, UK, were due mainly to local authority housing policies. And Wilson's study of African-American neighbourhoods with stable populations in Chicago suggests that high delinquency rates were due to a lack of parental control. Both these studies indicate that we cannot generalise from Shaw and McKay's research.

EVALUATION

The urban ecology of the Chicago School was concerned with the growth of cities, the development of distinctive neighbourhoods and the spatial distribution of different types of behaviour. Although its findings might only apply to a few American cities, the Chicago School has had an important influence on urban sociology. For example, its focus on the spatial distribution of criminal behaviour has provided direction for many research projects.

The Chicago School's emphasis on empirical research – first-hand observation and 'hard' data – has made a major contribution to sociological research methodology. Robert Park insisted his students got their 'pants dirty in real research'. He treated the city of Chicago like a research laboratory. His students developed both qualitative and quantitative research methods such as participant observation, case-study research, life histories and social surveys. This resulted in a number of classic sociological studies, including Frederic Thrasher's *The Gang* (1927) and Clifford Shaw's *The Jack Roller* (1930), a life history of a young street criminal.

BIOGRAPHY

Robert Park (1864-1944) was born in Harveyville, Pennsylvania. After graduating from the University of Michigan, he became a reporter focusing on city life, urban problems and direct observation of human behaviour. He became Professor of Sociology at the University of Chicago and President of the American Sociological Society.

QUESTIONS AND ANSWERS

Q1 A man is lying on the pavement, apparently unconscious. On another occasion, the same man is in the same position with an empty whisky bottle beside him. Why might people respond differently to the two situations?

A1 People respond in terms of the meanings they give to situations. In the first instance, they will probably see the man as ill, feel sympathetic, try to revive him and maybe call for an ambulance. In the second situation, they may define him as drunk, show little or no sympathy, and walk on by.

Q2 How does the idea of role-taking help to explain the views of the two tennis players in the foreground of the second picture?

A2 Role-taking involves putting yourself in the position of others and interpreting their responses. In this picture the tennis player on the other side of the net looks angry – he is scowling and shaking his fist. This can be seen as annoyance or as just fooling around. However, role-taking does not tell us which, if either, of these interpretations is correct.

Q3 How can role-taking help to develop a self-concept?

A3 Role-taking allows people to look at themselves either from the view of another person, or from an imaginary role they themselves are playing. When children play a make-believe role, seeing themselves in terms of this role helps them to develop a self-concept.

Q4 How do role-taking and self-awareness combine to develop people both as individuals and as members of society?

A4 As noted previously, role-taking helps to develop a self-concept. This is essential if people are to see themselves as individuals and act accordingly – in terms of their own goals. Role-taking also allows people to interpret the goals and actions of others and to be aware of what others expect from them. And this develops a person as a social being, as someone who can interact with others, as a member of society.

EVALUATION

Symbolic interaction focuses on small-scale interaction situations. Ideas such as role-taking and self-concept have provided important insights into the way people see themselves and others, and how this affects social interaction.

The focus on interaction situations has been seen as both a strength and a weakness. A strength , because of the insights it provides. A weakness, because it tends to ignore the wider society and issues such as inequalities of power and wealth.

BIOGRAPHY

George Herbert Mead (1863-1931) was one of the founders of symbolic interactionism. He saw the self as essentially social – it developed in a social context, it was shaped by meanings which directed social interaction. Born in Massachusetts, USA, Mead studied philosophy and social psychology and taught for many years at the University of Chicago. His students loved his lectures but Mead had great difficulty writing. Luckily, some of his students took excellent notes which formed the basis for his major work, *Mind, Self and Society* (1934), published after his death.

INTERACTION PROCESSES

QUESTIONS AND ANSWERS

Q1 Explain the concept of the looking-glass self.

A1 People interpret how others see them. It is like seeing a reflection in a mirror of how they think others view them. A person's picture of themselves comes, in part, from this perception – from their looking-glass self.

Q2 How does the self-fulfilling prophecy operate?

A2 A prophecy is a prediction of what is going to happen. A self-fulfilling prophecy is a prediction which comes to pass simply because it has been made. People tend to act in terms of the way they believe others see them – in terms of their looking-glass self. In this way, the prophecy – that they are intelligent, attractive or amusing – is likely to come to pass, to fulfil itself.

Q3 How does labelling operate?

A3 A label is a definition of a person applied by others. For example, teachers may label particular students as intelligent, hardworking and well-behaved or alternatively as underachieving, lazy and troublemakers. If the label 'sticks', other people tend to respond to the label. For example, if a person has a criminal record and has been labelled as an 'ex-con' then employers will tend to see them as untrustworthy and unreliable and not give then a job.

EVALUATION

The self-fulfilling prophecy is an interesting idea. However, studies applying it have produced mixed results. For example, *some* studies of children labelled by teachers as high and low achievers indicate a self-fulfilling prophecy – those defined as high achievers made greater progress even if there was no evidence to support the view that they were high achievers. However, similar studies found no evidence of a self-fulfilling prophecy.

Labelling theory has some evidence to support it. For example, the idea that 'deviant behaviour is behaviour that people so label' finds support from the following. In a low-income area, a brawl involving young people tends to be seen by police as evidence of delinquency. In a wealthy area, it is more likely to be seen as evidence of youthful high spirits. Working-class youth are more likely to be labelled as delinquent than their middle-class counterparts.

Critics of labelling theory argue that it tends to ignore the wider society, in particular inequalities of power. It often fails to ask questions such as: Who has the power to apply labels and make them stick? And: Why are some people more likely to receive negative labels and how does this relate to their position in society?

QUESTIONS AND ANSWERS

Q1 *Why does Goffman use the idea of performance in his analysis of social interaction?*

A1 According to Goffman, social interaction has many similarities with acting in a play. He sees social interaction as a series of 'theatrical performances' – we present ourselves to an audience in an attempt to give a believable performance, use suitable props and adopt appropriate mannerisms. In these respects we are like actors in a play. Goffman uses what has become known as the *dramaturgical analogy*.

Q2 *How can props contribute to an effective performance?*

A2 Props can help to make a performance believable by setting a tone, giving an impression, and defining a situation. Clothing provides an example. For instance, uniforms immediately indicate the part a person is playing – as a nurse, police person, soldier and so on. Furniture, décor and specialised equipment provide an appropriate setting for particular action. As the picture in Unit 15 indicates, the various props 'say' something to the audience. For example, the ribbon round the solicitor's papers doesn't just hold them together. It suggests they are important documents and sets them apart from and above ordinary papers.

Q3 *How does the idea of impression management help to explain Sister Mary Michael's performance?*

A3 Sister Mary Michael is managing the impression she is giving to her guest. She is dressed as a nun and is immediately recognisable as such. Her name suggests she is separate and different from women in the wider society. She has both a male and a female name which, along with her costume, suggests she should not be seen as a sexual being. The cross around her neck indicates she is a Christian. The setting is a convent – a place where nuns live and worship. All of the above combine to convey an impression both to insiders – the nuns – and to outsiders – the public – of who she is and what she stands for.

Q4 *Why does the patient see the doctor's performance as a failure?*

A4 People usually have views on how a person playing a part should look and act. In this case, the doctor, to use Goffman's theatrical comparison, would never win an Oscar. He is dressed in shorts and a Hawaiian shirt, and his feet are bare. He is smoking a cigar and drinking what appears to be a glass of whisky. Apart form his stethoscope, he looks like he should be on holiday. His manner – feet on the table and a greeting of 'Yo' – does not fit what most people expect from a doctor. And the setting is hardly appropriate for a doctor's surgery – a dartboard on the wall and a Dali-type lobster phone.

Judging by the patient's expression, the appearance and manner, activity and setting are nothing like what she expects. In this respect, the doctor's performance is judged to be unconvincing.

EVALUATION

Goffman has introduced some valuable concepts for the analysis of social interaction. Although there are obvious differences between actors on stage and people interacting in normal life, the framework provided by the concept of 'theatrical performance' has produced important insights.

Goffman recognises differences in power in interaction situations. For example, in *Asylums* (1968), he examines the unequal relationships between inmates and staff in a mental hospital. However, he does not widen the focus to society as a whole. As a result, he fails to examine society-wide inequalities, such as differences in wealth and income and their possible influence on small-scale interaction situations.

BIOGRAPHY

Erving Goffman (1922-1982) was born in Alberta, Canada. He completed his doctorate at the University of Chicago, became Professor of Sociology at the University of California and was elected President of the American Sociological Association. He died just before his presidential address. Goffman was recognised as a leading academic by the sociological establishment. He also achieved cult status as an original and distinctive thinker

ETHNOMETHODOLOGY

QUESTIONS AND ANSWERS

Q1 **What does the counselling experiment indicate about the methods people use to construct social reality?**

A1 The counselling experiment suggests that people construct sense where no sense exists. The answers provided by the 'counsellor' are random 'yes' and 'no' answers which bear no relation to the questions. Yet the students are determined to create sense and order. They do this by 'indexing' the answers in a particular context.

Q2 **What does the breaching experiment indicate about the way people make sense of the social world?**

A2 The breaching experiment shows that common understandings maintain an appearance of sense and order. When these common understandings are 'breached' or disrupted, people still try to impose sense and order. They do this by using the documentary method which assumes an underlying pattern, which is then used to make sense of the situation.

Q3 **What does Garfinkel mean when he states that the sense and order which people perceive in the social world may not actually exist?**

A3 Garfinkel claims that people construct social reality to impose sense and order on the social world. However, this sense and order may not actually exist. People construct it to make the social world appear knowable, reasonable and understandable.

EVALUATION

Most sociologists assume that social order has an objective reality – that it actually exists, and that it is orderly and patterned. Garfinkel provides a radical alternative to this view. From an ethnomethodological perspective, social order is a convenient fiction, an appearance of order and stability, an imposition of sense, a concoction of reality.

Ethnomethodology has come under a barrage of criticism from mainstream sociology. Critics have argued that it:

- Focuses on the trivial and insignificant, rather than the main issues of the day
- Ignores the wider society examining only small-scale interaction situations
- Fails to examine power differences and to consider that some may have the power to impose their constructions of reality on others.

Ethnomethodologists' criticisms of mainstream sociology has been redirected at them. If people construct sense and order, aren't ethnomethodologists doing exactly the same when they report the behaviour of others?

Despite these criticisms, ethnomethodology has raised important questions which challenge many of the assumptions of mainstream sociology.

BIOGRAPHY

Harold Garfinkel was born in Newark, New Jersey in 1917. He achieved a PhD in sociology at Harvard University. In 1954 he began a long teaching career at the University of California in Los Angeles from which he retired in 1987. His most famous work, *Studies in Ethnomethodology*, was published in 1967.

PHENOMENOLOGY

QUESTIONS AND ANSWERS

Q1 *On the basis of Atkinson's research what is:*
   a) A typical suicide death?
   b) A typical suicide biography?
   c) A common sense theory of suicide?

A1   a)   A type of death seen by coroners as typical of those who take their own lives. Such deaths include drowning, drug overdose, hanging and gassing.
   b)   A type of biography seen by coroners as typical of those who take their own lives. Aspects of such a biography include few if any friends and bouts of depression.
   c)   A common sense theory of suicide is a theory used by coroners to explain what they see as a suicide death. This theory makes use of the ideas of a typical suicide death and a typical suicide biography. It is a common sense theory because it is largely based on what seems reasonable and makes sense to most people.

Q2 *What does Atkinson mean when he says that there is no such thing as a 'real' or 'objective' suicide death?*

A2   From a phenomenological perspective, actions and events have no meaning in themselves. They only mean what people take them to mean. They have no reality outside these meanings. So, there is no 'real' or 'objective' suicide death. There is simply a meaning – suicide – which is applied to certain deaths.

EVALUATION

Phenomenology provides an important alternative to mainstream sociology. Some mainstream researchers claim that social isolation – for example, having no friends and living alone – is one of the main causes of suicide. From a phenomenological perspective, these researchers have simply uncovered the meanings used by coroners to classify a death as suicide. In particular, coroners see social isolation as part of the typical suicide biography. As a result, many officially defined suicide victims have experienced social isolation which then appears to be one of the causes of suicide.

Critics have argued that phenomenology leads nowhere. If the social world is simply a world of meaning, then the same applies not only to sociology in general but also to phenomenology. Phenomenologists are merely imposing their meanings on the social world.

Despite this criticism, phenomenology has had an important influence on sociology. It shows that sociologists must attend more closely to the meanings that people operate with. For example, such attention to meanings is essential to make sense of statistics on suicide, crime, unemployment, marriage, divorce, church attendance etc.

FEMINISM

QUESTIONS AND ANSWERS

Q1 *Why are liberal feminist demands referred to as reforms and those of Marxist feminists as revolutionary change?*

A1 Reform refers to changes within an existing system. Liberal feminists believe that equal rights can be achieved by new laws within the framework of the present society. Marxist feminists argue that fundamental change is needed to achieve equal rights. The whole system requires change from a capitalist to a communist society. This is revolutionary change.

Q2 *Briefly suggest some of the changes which might be required to end patriarchy.*

A2 Prioritise the policing and punishment of male violence against women, including rape and domestic violence. Condemn and eradicate forced marriage and female genital mutilation. Establish gender equality of power – for example, equal numbers of female and male MPs. Provide equality of access to positions of power and influence in areas such as the judiciary, business and religious organisations. Purge religions of prejudice and discrimination against women.

Q3 *How might Michelle Obama help to change stereotypes of African-American women?*

A3 As President Obama's wife, Michelle Obama is the 'first lady'. This is the first time an African-American woman has held this position. As a well-educated, confident, attractive wife and mother in a position of influence, Michelle Obama presents a positive image of womanhood. She has her own strongly held beliefs about many issues, including ecology and the care of children. The publicity given to her by the media may help change the largely negative stereotypes of African-American women.

Q4 *The postmodern view suggests that a united women's movement is unlikely. Discuss.*

A4 According to postmodernists, there is no universal essence of womanhood. Women as a group are characterised by their diversity rather than their similarity. This suggests that a united women's movement is unlikely.

EVALUATION

Postmodernism is one example of a new direction taken by some feminists in recent years. The idea of a universal experience of womanhood and a universal identity as a woman has been rejected. They have been seen as a creation of white, middle-class, heterosexual women who see all women sharing a common essence and a common experience.

Many feminists now see women as a diverse group with a range of different definitions of womanhood, different experiences, situations, cultures, ethnicities, classes and sexual orientations. As a result, women must define feminism for themselves and find their own identities. Instead of a single voice, there are many voices. However, the issues often remain the same. For example, gender violence remains a central issue for feminists today.

GENDER

QUESTIONS AND ANSWERS

Q1   *Briefly outline and assess the views that gender roles are based on a) biology and b) culture.*

A1   a)   Biological views state that differences in the biology of men and women account for differences in gender roles. George Peter Murdock's survey of 224 societies has been used to support this view. Murdock argues that biological differences have resulted in a tendency for strenuous tasks to be part of the male role and lighter, domestic tasks part of the female role. He claims that men's 'superior strength' and women's 'physiological burdens of pregnancy and nursing' lead to these differences in gender roles.

b)   Cultural views state that gender roles are shaped by culture – they are learned rather than biologically based. Evidence from a number of societies questions the view that differences in biology lead to differences in gender roles. In many traditional African societies women perform strenuous tasks such as farming, building huts and fetching water. In terms of the biological argument, these tasks are more suited to the male role.

Q2   *Discuss the view that gender should be seen as a range of variation rather than a simple male/female division.*

A2   Some cultures recognise a third gender. This may indicate that the male/female division may not provide an adequate classification of gender. Some researchers argue that gender is a range of variation. They see diversity rather than a straightforward male/female classification. They identify a variety of masculinities and femininities and mixtures of both.

EVALUATION

There is increasing evidence from a range of different societies of a wide variety of gender roles. Most researchers argue that this variety cannot be explained in terms of biological differences between males and females. Instead, gender is increasingly seen as a social construction, as a product of culture rather than biology.

There is also growing evidence of variation within society of so-called gender roles – for example, variations in sexual orientation. More and more people are 'coming out' and announcing their particular orientation. Researchers are increasingly recognising this diversity and seeing gender a range of variation, as a wide spectrum.

Some researchers argue that this variation is magnified by an increasing fluidity of gender roles. They see gender as fluid rather than fixed, with individuals redefining themselves rather than accepting an unchanging identity.

MICHEL FOUCAULT

QUESTIONS AND ANSWERS

Q1 *Until 1973, the American Psychiatric Association (APA) listed homosexuality as a psychological disorder. In 1973, the APA no longer classified homosexuality as a disorder. How can this be seen as a change in the discourse about homosexuality?*

A1 A discourse is a way of knowing , thinking about and understanding something. People base their actions on discourses. If homosexuality is defined and understood as an 'illness', then it follows that it should be 'treated' in order to 'cure' it. And when homosexuality was seen as a 'mental illness', it follows that it should be diagnosed and treated by psychiatrists – those trained to identify and treat psychological disorders. The official *declassification* of homosexuality as a 'mental illness' rejects this way of thinking about and dealing with homosexuality – it rejects the former discourse.

Q2 *With each new edition of its classification of psychological disorders, the APA deletes some old disorders and adds new ones. What support does this provide for Foucault's claim that psychiatrists are an extremely powerful group?*

A2 Defining what counts as a psychological disorder and diagnosing and treating a disorder can have an enormous effect on people's lives. It can make them feel better or worse. It can shape how they see themselves. It can influence how others behave towards them. And should they be seen to break the law, the criminal justice system recognises a diagnosis when deciding the outcome of a court case. Since psychiatrists define, diagnose and treat disorders, they are in an extremely powerful position in society.

EVALUATION

Foucault has been described as one of the greatest, most original and challenging thinkers of the 20th century. He developed an alternative to Marx's view of history and social change. Where Marx saw history as shaped by class conflict, Foucault saw history as a struggle between a variety of groups to impose their views on society – for example, the conflict between supporters of homeopathic medicine and conventional medicine. Such conflicts are based on discourses. And discourses regulate, discipline and control our thoughts and actions.

Foucault rejects the view that history can be seen as progress – that the development of medicine, science and democracy have advanced the human condition. History is simply the creation and replacement of discourses. For example, Foucault sees the various discourses on 'madness' as simply different, not better, not worse. He goes further stating that there is no objective measurement, no position of certainty on which to base a judgement. He has been criticised for this view as it implies that the world we live in is just a collection of discourses, no better, no worse than those that came before and will follow. And this applies to all academic subjects, including Foucault's own view of history.

MICHEL FOUCAULT

BIOGRAPHY

Michel Foucault was born in Poitiers, France in 1926. He achieved degrees in philosophy and psychology. His thesis on the history of 'madness' was first published in 1961. This was followed by a series of publications including *The Birth of the Clinic: An Archaeology of Medical Perception* (1975), *Discipline and Punish: The Birth of the Prison* (1979) and *The History of Sexuality* (Volumes 1-3, 1980-85).

In 1970, Foucault was elected to a position at the prestigious College de France where he taught the History of Systems of Thought. In the late 1970s and early 1980s he lectured at the University of California. Throughout his life, Foucault participated in 'limit experiences' – pushing himself to the limit, for example experimenting with LSD, a powerful hallucinogenic drug. He believed that such experiences led to increased awareness and intellectual breakthroughs. Foucault died in Paris in 1984, aged 57.

PIERRE BOURDIEU

QUESTIONS AND ANSWERS

Q1 *How might the cultural, social, economic and symbolic capitals of the family in Picture 1 work together to keep them at the top of the class system?*

A1 The capitals of the family will probably combine to maintain their class position. If one type of capital is high, then the others tend to be high. They often reinforce each other. For example, if social capital is high then it may provide valuable contacts who offer job opportunities which increase economic capital. And honours such as an MBE will tend to increase social status which may lead to a corresponding increase in social capital.

The father in the picture is using his social capital to advise his daughter on her education. And the son is off to a Picasso exhibition in line with the high cultural capital of the family. In all probability, the high capitals of the parents will be passed to their children who will continue to enjoy their position at the top of the class system.

Q2 *How might high capitals have contributed to David Cameron's and George Osborne's route to the top?*

A2 Both David Cameron and George Osborne were born in to high capital families. Their parents were rich – they could afford to pay for their children to attend expensive, fee-paying, public schools. Both went to Oxford University, one of the top universities in the UK. At Oxford they were both members of the exclusive Bullingdon dining club. Their schools, university and social life brought valuable contacts, many of whom they retain today. The cultural capital provided by their families and their education has served them well. They probably feel confident and at home in a cabinet where most members share their background and advantages.

Q3 *According to Bourdieu, how does education reproduce the established order?*

A3 Bourdieu argues that education is based on the culture of the 'dominant classes'. Children from these classes have more of this culture. As a result, they are more likely to succeed in the educational system. In particular, their cultural capital gives them a head start in the early years of primary school.

Middle-class mothers have more cultural, social and economic capital than working-class mothers. They use these capitals to further their children's education – by providing more help with homework, paying for extra tuition and using their contacts to select schools.

Young people from wealthy families who have gone to public schools are more likely to choose elite universities such as Oxford and Cambridge. Growing up with greater capitals gives them more confidence and the belief that they deserve the best.

Cultural, social and economic capitals are not evenly distributed. Those at the top of the class system have most, those at the bottom have least. These inequalities are reflected in educational attainment – in general, the children of the dominant classes obtain the highest qualifications. Education is one of the ways in which advantages are passed from one generation to the next. In Bourdieu's words, the role of education is 'the reproduction of the established order'.

EVALUATION

Pierre Bourdieu was one of the most influential sociologists of the late 20th century. His main focus was on social inequality and its reproduction. He directed attention back to social class at a time when it was going out of fashion. His work on education influenced a number of British sociologists including Stephen J. Ball, Diane Reay and Miriam E. David.

Critics argue that Bourdieu paid too much attention to social structure and its reproduction and too little to how that structure could be changed. His critics claim that he pictured people behaving in terms of the structure of society rather than exercising choice, shaping their own social world and acting to change society.

BIOGRAPHY

Pierre Bourdieu was born in France in a mountain village in the Pyrenees. He served in the army in French colonial Algeria and his first book, *The Algerians*, was published in 1958. He studied under the Marxist philosopher Louis Althusser. In 1964, he was appointed to the Ecoles de Haute Etudes en Sciences Sociales where he set up the Centre for the Sociology of Education and Culture. In 1981, he became Chair of Sociology at the prestigious College of France. Bourdieu wrote over 30 books including *Distinction: A Social Critique of the Judgement of Taste* (1979) and *Sociology in Question* (1993).

POSTMODERN SOCIETY

QUESTIONS AND ANSWERS

Q1 *How might multiple realities make life seem meaningless?*

A1 Multiple realities provide different views of the world, different norms and different values. This diversity can challenge our existing reality and lead us to question our present norms and values. It can threaten established meanings and our views of the truth. As a result, we might question everything and life might appear meaningless.

Q2 *Suggest why there may have been a loss of faith in science, medicine and technology.*

A2 When experts in science, medicine and technology present a variety of often contradictory viewpoints, people tend to lose faith in their expertise and question their objectivity. Faced with experts disagreeing, most people have insufficient knowledge to make an informed judgement.

Q3 *Why are New Age religions and complementary medicine becoming increasingly popular?*

A3 In the absence of one truth, one reality, one view of the world, it becomes more difficult to arrive at definite answers. This opens the door to a range of alternatives such as New Age religions and complementary medicine. Without a means of judging the truth and worth of either the traditional or the new, the new alternatives are more readily accepted.

Q4 *How can themed hotels in Las Vegas and blues music on Beale Street be seen as examples of hyperreality?*

A4 Hyperreality blurs the line between reality and illusion, between simulation and the real thing. Illusion – something which is not real, not the true state of affairs – becomes something real and true. Simulations – imitations or copies of something – become the real thing. The themed hotels in Las Vegas simulate aspects of New York, Paris and Luxor. In one respect they are not real. In another respect they are – many people have a sense of these cities when they stay in the hotels. In this instance, the line between reality and illusion is blurred.
Beale Street, 'the home of the blues' is 50 years past its heyday. It has been recreated for tourists with 'blues bars', 'blues cafes', 'blues record shops', 'blues memorabilia' and 'blues music' blaring from clubs and bars along the street. This is music mainly for white tourists – blues is largely dead and gone in black communities. As such, it can be seen as hyperreality – it has little depth, it is a second-rate copy, it merely simulates. Yet many people think they are listening to the real thing – the 'real deal'.

EVALUATION

This unit has illustrated aspects of postmodern society as seen by sociologists who call themselves postmodernists. It has not dealt directly with *postmodernism* – the more general theory adopted by postmodernists. This theory contains some of the features they see as characteristic of postmodern society. Here is an example.

Some postmodernists claim that there is no objective way, no yardstick, to establish truth and falsity. As a result, we cannot be certain about anything. Critics have argued that if this is the case, then it can be applied to the findings of postmodernists.

Postmodernists see a clear break between modern and postmodern society. However, most sociologists now see today's society as a development of modernity, as a new phase or new stage of modern society.

Despite criticisms, postmodernists' views of postmodern society have had an important influence on sociologists' pictures of 'late modernity', 'second modernity', 'liquid modernity' and 'reinvention society'.

LATE MODERNITY

QUESTIONS AND ANSWERS

Q1 *Giddens compares living in late modernity to a ride on a juggernaut.*
   a) *What has the juggernaut smashed through?*
   b) *Where is it going?*
   c) *According to the flags, what does the journey provide?*
   d) *What emotions does it arouse?*

A1 a) Habit, tradition and continuity.
   b) The unknown.
   c) Rapid change, risk and uncertainty.
   d) Excitement, exhilaration, fear, concern.

Q2 a) *What does Giddens mean by reflexive?*
   b) *Why are people becoming increasingly reflexive?*

A2 a) Reflexive means reflecting on – looking back on the self, social relationships and society.
   b) Society in late modernity is rapidly changing. Because of this the self is no longer clearly defined and custom and tradition no longer provide clear directions for behaviour. As a result, people reflect on their identity, question their behaviour and choose from a range of possible alternatives. Late modernity is a high risk society. As a result, people question the trust they are asked to place in those appointed to deal with these risks.

Q3 *How might the concept of confluent love help to explain the fragility of intimate relationships, such as marriage and partnerships, in late modern society?*

A3 Giddens argues that confluent love provides the basis for intimate relationships such as marriage and partnerships in late modern society. Without it there is little else to hold intimate relationships together.

Maintaining the deep emotional closeness that confluent love demands is not easy over long periods of time. In late modernity, people are less likely to follow traditional norms which define marriage as a lifelong commitment. And they are more likely to reflect on their relationship and abandon it, should it not live up to hopes and expectations based on confluent love.

EVALUATION

Critics have argued that Giddens has exaggerated the differences between late modernity and earlier phases of modernity. In particular, they state that tradition continues to be an important factor directing people's behaviour. And, in Giddens' (2009) words,

> 'Some critics have argued that I see reflexivity as a wholly positive development, reflecting the opening up of social life to more choice. However, such reflexivity could also be leading to heightened levels of "anomie", as described by Durkheim, and in that sense, reflexivity may be more of a problem to be solved than a welcome element to be promoted.'

Some critics have argued that Giddens has placed too much emphasis on confluent love as the basis of intimate relationships. They point to the importance of home-building and raising children in many relationships. Despite these criticisms, Giddens' views have inspired many sociologists. He notes that,

> 'The ideas I have developed have been taken in fruitful directions by other sociologists and, in that sense, it is satisfying to have provided a theoretical framework and some conceptual tools for younger generations to take forward and develop.'

BIOGRAPHY

Born in 1938 in Edmonton, London, Anthony Giddens is regarded as one of the world's foremost sociologists. He studied sociology and psychology at Hull University, gained a Masters at LSE and a PhD at King's College, Cambridge. He became a professor at Cambridge in 1987 and from 1997 to 2003, he was director of the LSE. He was an advisor to the former British prime minister, Tony Blair, and was given a life peerage in 2004. As Baron Giddens, he sits on the Labour benches in the House of Lords. He has written over 30 books including, *Capitalism and Modern Social Theory* (1971); *Modernity and Self-Identity* (1991); *The Third Way* (1998); *Runaway World* (1999) and *Sociology* (6th edition, 2009).

QUESTIONS AND ANSWERS

Q1 *Beck argues that the risks in the second modernity are largely human-made. Briefly comment on this view with reference to the first four pictures.*

A1 Processed foods are human-made. The producers are aware of the risks to health. Information about these risks is available to those who eat processed foods. Nuclear power stations are human-made and there is plenty of information about the risks of producing nuclear energy. The pollution of land, sea and air is largely the result of human activity. Information about these risks and how to reduce them is readily available. The job market and social relationships are human creations, as are the risks involved. Since the above risks are human-made, risk-monitoring, risk-management and risk-reduction can be placed under human control.

Q2 *Beck states that, 'I is becoming the social structure of second modern society itself'. Yet he does not see the second modernity as a 'me-first society'. Discuss, using the ideas of altruistic individualism and cooperative individualism.*

A2 Beck argues that people cannot live a totally self-centred life. They cannot completely operate as 'I' and completely focus on 'me'. They need some form of friendship and support in order to live as an individual. And this only comes with a concern for others and a degree of unselfishness – in other words, with altruism.

This approach is particularly important in partnerships based on love. To sustain this type of relationship, people must share a life together *and* have a life of their own. Beck calls this cooperative individualism.

EVALUATION

Beck claims that compared to pre-industrial society, risks today are more likely to be human-made, that people are more aware of them, and more able to calculate the degree of danger involved. Critics argue that Beck has underestimated the extent and awareness of risk in pre-industrial society – for example, widespread diseases such as bubonic plagues, devastating harvest failures and resulting famines, high levels of infant mortality, and wars.

Beck argues that in Western Europe and North America 'the struggle for one's "daily bread" has lost its urgency' – the poor are no longer starving. Today's risks, such as global warming and nuclear accidents, affect rich and poor alike. As a result, the significance of social class has declined and people are less likely to identify with class. In an individualistic society, they are concerned about risks as individuals rather than as members of a social class.

Critics argue that Beck has overstated his case. In recent years the gap between rich and poor in terms of income and wealth has widened in Western society. People's class position still has an important effect on their life chances and the way they experience risk. For example, those in lower classes are more likely to be unemployed and unemployment can be cushioned with money; the moneyed class are more able to avoid risks – for instance, moving away from polluted areas. As Alan Scott *in Risk Society or Angst Society* (2000) argues, 'Money can give far more protection from risks'.

BIOGRAPHY

Ulrich Beck was born in Germany in 1944. He studied sociology, philosophy, psychology and political science at Munich University. He became professor of sociology at a number of German universities. In 1992, he became director of the Institute of Sociology at Munich University and in 1997 he became the British Journal of Sociology Professor at the London School of Economics. His publications include *Risk Society* (1992), *Individualisation* (2001) (with his wife, Elisabeth Beck-Gernsheim) and *World at Risk* (2008).

LIQUID MODERNITY

QUESTIONS AND ANSWERS

Q1 **Why does Bauman compare life in liquid modernity with walking in a minefield?**

A1 Walking in a minefield is uncertain, insecure and anxious. So, according to Bauman, is life in liquid modernity. Relationships are unstable, jobs are insecure, and nothing is certain.

Q2 **Why does Bauman see work in liquid modernity as no longer providing a secure basis for identities and life projects?**

A2 In Bauman's words, 'Working life is saturated with insecurity' in liquid modernity. With short-term contracts, rolling contracts, redundancy and retraining becoming more common, jobs for life are largely a thing of the past. As a result, people are less likely to base their identity on their occupation – which may regularly change. They are also less likely to rely on work – an increasingly insecure source of income – to fund their life-projects such as buying a house.

Q3 a) **What are 'top pocket relationships'?**

    b) **Why, according to Bauman, are they a feature of liquid modernity?**

A3 a) A 'top pocket relationship' is a fairly loose relationship which can be called upon and activated when required.

    b) In liquid modernity, there is a conflict between individual freedom and the need for security. This places a strain on relationships and has led to an increase in separations. 'Top pocket relationships' have developed in response to this situation. The bonds have to be 'loosely tied so they can be untied with little delay' should the relationship prove unsatisfactory.

Q4 a) **How can individualisation lead to self-blame?**

    b) **Why are poor and powerless people more likely to blame themselves?**

A4 a) Individualisation means that people tend to rely on themselves and create their own identities. As a result, if things go wrong, they will tend to blame themselves rather than others, their class position or society.

    b) Poor and powerless people have fewer resources to deal with failure. As a result, they find it more difficult to improve their situation and boost their identity, and they are more likely to blame themselves.

EVALUATION

Zygmunt Bauman is widely recognised as an important social theorist. His books are fresh, exciting and bursting with ideas. He paints a fascinating picture of liquid modernity. His picture is painted in broad brushstrokes and sometimes lacks hard evidence to support it. However, he has put forward a range of interesting ideas for others to research and develop.

As with many sociologists, Bauman has been criticised for overstating his case. For example, Anthony Elliott *in Contemporary Social Theory* (2009) argues that Bauman's examples of liquid modernity are drawn largely from the West rather than from other parts of the world. And he tends to neglect the many ways that so-called liquid modern societies are still based on the traditions and world views of modernity.

BIOGRAPHY

Zygmunt Bauman was born in Poland in 1925. He studied sociology at the Warsaw Academy of Social Sciences and philosophy at the University of Warsaw. He moved to England in 1971, partly as a result of the anti-Semitism experienced by his Jewish parents. He became Professor of Sociology at both the University of Leeds and the University of Warsaw. Bauman has written over 50 books including *Liquid Modernity* (2000/2012), *Liquid Love* (2003), *Liquid Lives* (2005), *Liquid Times* (2007), and *Culture in a Liquid Modern World* (2011).

GLOBALISATION

QUESTIONS AND ANSWERS

Q1 *Multinational corporations are a significant part of the process of globalisation. Discuss with reference to Picture 1.*

A1 The picture shows three multinational corporations – McDonald's, Coca-Cola and Nike – in four separate countries. The picture gives only a small indication of the global penetration of these corporations. As the caption states, multinationals account for more than two-thirds of global trade. In terms of Giddens' definition, the activities of multinationals involve the coming together of 'social, cultural and economic factors' across the world.

Q2 *What evidence does the map provide for the globalisation of finance?*

A2 The map shows eight of the many stock exchanges spanning the globe. This means that shares can be traded 24 hours a day and the price of shares will be determined by world trading. In this respect, financial transactions are global.

Q3 *What do the organisations shown in Picture 3 suggest about globalisation?*

A3 Three of the organisations – the United Nations, World Bank and International Monetary Fund – are global. Their logos represent the world. Most of the world's countries are members. (There are probably 196 countries in the world, though estimates vary slightly.) The other three organisations – the European Union, the African Union and the Arab League – are regional. They indicate that individual countries are forming larger organisations which may become increasingly global in membership.

Q4 *Why do some researchers see globalisation as cultural imperialism?*

A4 Many transnational corporations are Western and many are from the United States. Their products circle the globe. This has been seen as Western cultural imperialism or, as the picture of Mr America suggests, as Americanisation. The West has had a major influence on the tastes of the world. Rap is now a global music, footballers are world stars and James Bond movies are shown on every continent. Western fashions are now global fashions in the world's major cities. However, it is not just one-way traffic from the West to the rest of the world. Tastes in food provide an example to the contrary – chicken tikka masala is the UK's favourite dish.

Q5 *How can the idea of glocalisation be used to counter the idea of cultural imperialism?*

A5 Glocalisation refers to a mixing of cultures in which the local and the global meet and something new is created. This suggests that local cultures are not swept away by cultural imperialism. Instead, they select from the rest of the world and shape what they find to their tastes. So, although Bollywood – the Indian film industry – is influenced by Hollywood, its output is clearly Indian, based on local Indian culture and appealing to a mainly Indian audience.

Q6 **Why does Beck argue that many of today's risks are global and can only be dealt with by global organisations?**

A6 Pollution, climate change and over-fishing know no national boundaries. They are global risks produced by, and posing a threat to, countries across the world. As such, they require global solutions. According to Beck, the most effective way to reduce global risks is to develop global organisations with the power to deal with them.

Q7 **How can globalisation present alternative views which challenge traditional ways?**

A7 Globalisation involves global communication via the Internet, TV, films, music and international travel. This results in a variety of views and values being spread across the world. This variety can challenge existing traditions and may result in detraditionalisation – the replacement of established traditions.

EVALUATION

The idea of globalisation has entered everyday life – it is regularly talked about by broadcasters, politicians and business people. And it forms a part of every topic in sociology from education and crime to family and religion. Some idea of the scope of globalisation is provided by the title of the following book – *Fifty Key Thinkers in Globalisation* (Coleman and Sajed, 2013).

This unit has provided a very brief introduction to globalisation. However, it touches some of the key issues and offers a starting point for further reading.

THE NETWORK SOCIETY

QUESTIONS AND ANSWERS

Q1 **According to Castells, what is new about the network society?**

A1 Social networks are as old as humankind. In recent years they have been transformed by digital communication. Social networks are increasingly digital networks. And digital networks are global – they know no boundaries. As a result, the network society is a global society.

Q2 **Why are poor people increasingly drawn into global crime networks?**

A2 Across the world the gap between rich and poor is widening. Poor people are largely excluded from global economic networks and the wealth they generate. One response to exclusion is to create an alternative economic global network – a global crime network. Illegal drug networks provide an example. Many of those involved are drawn from poor people, the powerless and the excluded.

Q3 **Why is Castells optimistic about the contribution of digital networks to social movements?**

A3 Castells believes that many social movements benefit humankind. They aim to promote freedom, democracy and equality of opportunity; they turn 'fear into outrage and outrage into hope for a better humanity'. Digital communications have played a major part in many recent social movements – they have helped to create and organise networks of protest. For example, in the Tunisian revolution Twitter, Facebook, YouTube, websites and smart phones were used to record, publicise and organise demonstrations.

EVALUATION

Manuel Castells has produced the first major sociological study of digital communication in a global context. His three volume publication *The Information Age: Economy, Society and Culture* (2nd edition, 2000) is packed with data and new ideas. Translated into over 10 languages, it has become *the* work on the subject. A review in *The Economist* describes Castells as 'the first significant philosopher of cyberspace'.

While praising Castells' 'brilliant insights', Anthony Elliot *in Contemporary Social Theory* (2009) claims that he has overstated the significance of digital networks. Elliot argues that although Castells recognises that such networks can exclude, there is a tendency for him to neglect 'the many millions of disconnected from our age of informationalism'. Digital communication may not blanket the world to the extent that Castells claims.

BIOGRAPHY

Manuel Castells was born in Barcelona in 1942. He achieved a PhD in sociology from the University of Paris. He is Emeritus Professor of Sociology at the University of California, where he taught for 24 years. He has been presented with 15 Doctorates from universities across the world, taught in 20 universities, and received a number of international awards. He has written and edited more than 20 books, including *The Information Age: Economy, Society and Culture* (Volumes 1-3, second edition, 2000), *The Network Society: A Cross Cultural Perspective* (2004), and *Networks of Outrage and Hope: Social Movements in the Internet Age* (2012).

QUESTIONS AND ANSWERS

Q1 *According to Anthony Elliott, 'the self becomes a site for endless improvement' in the reinvention society. Give examples of this process from the picture of the 'Reinvention Mall'.*

A1 Buying new and fashionable clothes is an obvious example of transforming and improving the presentation of self. Diets and personal trainers promise to resculpt, remould and enhance the body. Cosmetic dentistry, cosmetic surgery and makeovers provide opportunities to redesign, reconstruct and improve appearance. Therapy offers a 'new you' with a positive and dynamic outlook. Self-help provides a recipe for self-improvement. And speed dating offers possibilities for a fresh start and a new and improved relationship.

Q2 *Why is adaptability and continuous updating of skills needed in the reinvention society?*

A2 The job market is constantly changing. People are increasingly hired for one-off projects on short-term contracts. As a result, they must learn new skills, 'embrace change' and adapt their careers to meet new demands and fresh opportunities.

Q3 *Why must corporations constantly reinvent themselves and their products?*

A3 Corporations operate in a global economy which is increasingly competitive. Because of this they must produce new and improved products. And they must restructure in order to meet the demands of a rapidly changing global economy. They must therefore constantly reinvent themselves if they are to survive and prosper.

EVALUATION

In his short, entertaining and illuminating book *Reinvention*, Anthony Elliott draws together the ideas of sociologists such as Giddens and Bauman and takes them a step further. He links the personal and the global, examining how individuals respond to global processes. In particular, he looks at how the demands of globalisation for endless reinvention, transformation and improvement shape individuals' priorities, emotions and concerns.

BIOGRAPHY

Anthony Elliott took his degrees at the Universities of Melbourne, Australia and Cambridge, UK, where his supervisor was Anthony Giddens. From 1999-2004 he was the Foundation Director of the Centre for Critical Theory at the University of the West of England, from 2004-2006 he was Professor of Sociology at the University of Kent, and from 2006-2012 he was Chair of Sociology at Flinders University, Australia. In 2012 he became Director of the Hawke Research Institute at the University of South Australia.

Elliott has written and edited some 30 books, including *Contemporary Social Theory* (2009), *The New Individualism* (with Charles Lemert, 2009), *Mobile Lives* (with John Urry, 2010), *On Society* (with Bryan S.Turner, 2012) and *Reinvention* (2013).

COMMON SENSE

QUESTIONS AND ANSWERS

Q1 *Briefly suggest the reasoning on which the common sense statements were based. These statements were made in 1949 so some intelligent guesswork may be needed.*

A1 a) The southern states of the USA have higher temperatures than the northern states. Common sense suggests that soldiers from the southern states would be better able to cope with the hot climate of the South Pacific.

b) War is dangerous. Wartime living conditions are often very unpleasant. This suggests that soldiers would be more eager to return home during the war than after the war ended.

c) Soldiers with less education would probably have experienced more hardship in civilian life than their better educated counterparts. As a result, it might be expected that they would be better able to cope with the hardships of war.

d) In 1949, stereotypes of African Americans pictured them as less ambitious and less able than white Americans. In terms of this stereotype, African Americans would be less likely to want promotion.

Q2 *What does this study suggest about sociology and common sense?*

A2 Sociology has sometimes been dismissed as common sense dressed up in fancy language. Its findings have been seen as obvious – things that everybody knows. This research rejects these views. It shows the dangers of relying on common sense. It shows that common sense can be nonsense. It makes the case for sociological research.